THE BASICS OF

QUALITY
AUDITING

RONALD BLANK

CRC Press
Taylor & Francis Group
Boca Raton London New York

CRC Press is an imprint of the
Taylor & Francis Group, an **informa** business

CRC Press
Taylor & Francis Group
6000 Broken Sound Parkway NW, Suite 300
Boca Raton, FL 33487-2742

© 1999 by Ronald Blank
CRC Press is an imprint of Taylor & Francis Group, an Informa business

No claim to original U.S. Government works

ISBN 13: 978-0-527-76355-8 (pbk)

Visit the Taylor & Francis Web site at
http://www.taylorandfrancis.com

and the CRC Press Web site at
http://www.crcpress.com

Library of Congress Cataloging-in-Publication Data

Catalog record is available from the Library of Congress

Table of Contents

Introduction

The increasing number of quality systems in industry and in the service sectors that are or are becoming ISO 9000 compliant has caused both a corresponding increase in the amount of quality auditing performed and a change in the way quality auditing is used. No longer is quality auditing merely a policing action or a method for obtaining more information about a supplier. Auditing has developed as a real quality improvement tool. The traditional basic audit questions such as, "Do you have a procedure?" and "Are you following the procedure?" have been supplemented by two more equally important questions, namely, "Does the procedure actually meet your needs?" and "What needs to happen to improve the quality of your output?"

This book is about the basics of auditing. It will give the reader a sufficient knowledge and understanding of quality auditing so that the reader can perform valid and effective audits that answer these four questions. It is the author's intent to both instruct the reader and to present quality auditing as a useful management tool.

In addition, the appendix contains sample audit forms that may be used as models by the reader for developing his own specific forms.

CHAPTER 1

Why Perform Quality Audits?

Although a quality audit can be defined as a "planned, independent, and documented assessment to determine whether agreed-upon requirements are being met" (*Certified Quality Auditor Brochure*, American Society for Quality), the specific reasons for performing this type of audit will vary from each organization. The eight main reasons are to ensure:

- System compliance
- Procedures are followed
- Activities are recorded
- Compliance to contracts and specifications
- The evaluation of products and services
- Process compliance
- Effectiveness of quality system
- Opportunities for improvement are illustrated

These eight reasons are discussed in more detail in the following sections. In addition, audits are not designed or intended to criticize or assign blame. They are to help management manage. An auditor is the eyes and ears of the quality system. The audit report is a communication tool to inform management of the realities within the company. Audit reports are often the triggers that initiate product or process improvement, corrective actions, and procedure updates.

Ensure System Compliance

Traditionally, a quality audit is a means of verifying compliance to the quality system, the contract and specifications, and process instructions. A quality audit answers two questions: Do you have written documentation and are you following it? Compliance means that the written documentation is being followed. An auditor verifying compliance to the system would review the written quality procedures and the records generated by the procedure when it was performed. The records are evidence that the procedure was followed and that contract and specification compliance and process compliance were similarly verified.

Modern quality auditing is a break with tradition because it requires not only verification of compliance to the documentation, but also verification of the effectiveness of the procedure. An auditor not only checks that there is a written procedure and it is being followed, but also checks that it is producing the intended results and is effective in fulfilling the goal of the procedure. Procedures in need of revision will be less effective if complied with strictly. An audit can be an effective indicator of when a procedure needs to be updated.

Ensure Procedures Are Followed

Quality and consistency result from correctly following established procedures. Audits are performed to verify that procedures are correctly and consistently followed. A procedure tells who does what, when, and where. An instruction tells how. They may be all on one document or separate documents. To verify that the procedure is being followed, the auditor must ask these questions:

- Who is supposed to do it?
- What are they supposed to do?
- When are they supposed to do it?
- Where are they supposed to do it?
- How are they supposed to do it?

Written documentation describing a process that does not answer all five of these questions is incomplete. An auditor would make note of this in the audit report. The audit report would say, "documentation requires further development" or similar words to that effect. One would question how effective the written procedure could be if it never tells when or where it applies.

Ensure Activities Are Recorded

The purpose of an audit may be to ensure there are adequate records that the procedure was performed. Such records take a variety of forms including written forms to be filled out, videotapes, photographs, computer printouts, etc. A procedure should indicate how the records should be kept. Auditors check the records indicated by the procedure. The auditor should be able to tell from the records that the procedure was followed. If the auditor cannot determine this from the records, then the records are inadequate. While the records are evidence that the procedure was followed, they are also data that can be analyzed by engineering or management. These records provide the audit trail.

Sequentially numbered forms or forms issued by a specific person often indicate a "logbook." The logbook must be mentioned in the system documentation. Sometimes a particular departmental activity may be recorded in a logbook that is unofficial and not mentioned in the system documentation. These unofficial records can often carry more credibility with certain employees than official records. An unofficial logbook may exist whenever form or record numbers are assigned, but nothing in the procedure describes how the number is assigned or even that they are supposed to be numbered. In this case, a need for the unofficial logbook exists because that logbook is the only way to track the records. The procedure should be changed to authorize the logbook. Whereas if the procedure already says the forms are supposed to be numbered, tells how the numbers are assigned, and used for traceability, then an unofficial logbook is unnecessary. In that case, the logbook is an unauthorized, uncontrolled document used to control records. Corrective action is necessary here. In a well-documented system that requires adequate records, an unofficial logbook may be nothing more than a habit or an indication of someone's insecurity. If the logbook contains any information that is not contained in the official records, then the official records are either inadequate or the personnel not properly trained to rely on them. Either case is reason for corrective action.

All procedures produce results when followed. Verifying the existence of these results is evidence of compliance to the procedure. The records required are results, but results are not limited to records. Whenever possible, verify physical results that are not records and see if they agree with the records. Here is an example: A procedure says to package a part a certain way. The written records for the process indicate that lot number 7123-AB-1998 of that part has been packaged by employee J. Smith on Feb. 19, but not yet shipped. Examine the parts of that lot number and see if they have been packaged properly and that the packaging took place on that day by J. Smith. All records must agree with physical results.

Ensure Compliance to Contracts and Specifications

When evaluating a supplier, examine the method a company uses to identify its customer expectations and communicate them to the necessary departments. In an audit of contract review activities, investigate how an order or contract is reviewed to determine if the customer's requirements are adequately defined, documented, and communicated properly. Ideally, there should be a means of resolving differences between interpretations of requirements and a means of determining that the company has the capability to fulfill the requirements of the order or contract. This contributes to the "no surprises" way of doing business and prevents problems down the road.

An internal audit of a contract review is a verification that such a review has taken place and any differences have been resolved. This is such an important activity for proper quality planning and fulfillment of quality policy that the audit should not be taken lightly. The audit verifies that the contract is properly reviewed and can be executed. The contract review enables proper quality planning and fulfillment of the quality policy.

To ensure that the requirements of the contract and applicable specifications are being fulfilled is the role of inspection and testing. To adhere to specifications and contracts is actually to comply with them. Therefore, when verifying compliance, an audit may include inspection. When this is done, the inspection sample size is often reduced. In rare cases it may be that the auditor's purpose is more to establish the authenticity and credibility of the inspection records than to verify product conformance.

Auditing an ISO 9001 system requires that the effectiveness of the system be determined. Process control is part of the system. Therefore, the main reason for verifying contract and specification compliance is to check the effectiveness of the process controls that are in place. A manufacturing process that is not controlled effectively is more likely to produce product that does not meet the applicable specifications.

Ensure the Evaluation of Products and Services

An effective quality system will produce products or services that are in compliance with the contract and specifications. The less effective the system is, the more likely you will find products or services that do not comply with the requirements.

Dock audits and customer service records provide real evidence of the effectiveness of the system as a whole. In a dock audit you see the product, as the customer will be receiving it. Almost every aspect of the quality system in one way or another has an effect on product in this condition. Higher than expected defect rates, or the same defect occurring repeatedly, is evidence that some part of the quality system is not effective. Dock audits are also a convenient time to check product identification and traceability, as well as handling, storage, packaging, preservation, and delivery practices.

In customer service the same problem showing up again and again is evidence that the system has not been effective in treating or preventing that particular quality problem.

Ensure Process Compliance

A manufacturing process is a planned sequence of events producing the intended product at the intended quality. Compliance with the procedures is usually verified during the audits of their respective parts of the quality system. However, these procedures are not isolated, unrelated activities. They are integrated into one overall manufacturing process. It is by auditing the manufacturing or service process as a whole that you can evaluate the effectiveness of the integration. You can see how these procedures relate to each other, how they feed to and from each other, and how they work together to produce product.

Evaluating system effectiveness is not the only benefit. Process audits answer the question: Is the manufacturing process taking place in the prescribed manner? The objective eye of an auditor can identify things that people close to the process can easily miss. Identification and improvement of opportunities for mis-processing can prevent defects and servicing errors before they become problems.

Ensure Effectiveness of Quality System

ISO 9000 standards specifically require that audits determine the effectiveness of the quality system and that follow-up activities include verifying the effectiveness of corrective actions taken. These two requirements provide reasons to audit that go beyond mere system compliance. They force the auditor to examine if the company is making progress toward achieving the goals outlined in the quality policy. In addition, they require the auditor to verify that corrective actions taken actually solve the problem for which they were implemented.

Every procedure should have a stated purpose and scope. When reviewing the documentation, the auditor should ask two questions. Does this purpose contribute to quality or meet some need that the company has? Does the scope fully encompass everything necessary to fulfill the purpose? After meeting with the people who carry out the procedure, the auditor determines how they are performing the procedure and obtains evidence that the procedure was actually done. The auditor should review the evidence and ask this question: Did the procedure fulfill its purpose or was the company's need met? If the procedure was effective in fulfilling the purpose, then it has merit. Next the auditor should ask: Can the procedure be improved? Improvements can be anything that make the procedure more effective, less costly, less resource consuming, more error resistant, etc.

A good evaluation of the merit of a procedure can tell you if the procedure itself is defective or lacking. In this way, an audit can help uncover the root cause of a problem.

Just as an audit can evaluate a procedure, it can also be used to evaluate a product. It was pointed out earlier how an audit may include inspection. Note that an auditor must not audit his own work or his own department. This objectivity allows auditors to see things that people who handle the product or perform the service every day do not see. An internal auditor can be a useful pair of eyes and ears to judge product quality. Furthermore, product quality is an indicator of the effectiveness of the procedures. Inspection and test procedures should identify defects before the product is packaged. Process control procedures should prevent defects from occurring in the first place. An evaluation of the product merit can tell you how effective these are.

Ensure Opportunities for Improvement

The objectivity of auditors makes them especially adept at finding opportunities for improvement. Auditors coming from other departments have a less biased perspective. They have no work habits related to the procedure. They should look for ways to improve procedures and discuss them with the responsible managers or supervisors. The auditor may mention a suggestion agreed upon in the audit report so the suggestion cannot be forgotten or ignored. If there are no opportunities for improvement the auditor need not fret, as important opportunities for improvement, if present, are somewhat obvious. The less obvious ones are often less important.

Sometimes an audit may be done specifically to find opportunities for improvement. This is one case of how auditing can help determine corrective actions to existing problems. While ISO 9000 standards require scheduled audits of procedures, nothing in it forbids unscheduled audits to help solve problems or prevent defects.

Verifying mere compliance to the system is not the only goal of an audit. A second reason is to evaluate the effectiveness of the procedures. There is even a third reason. An audit should identify opportunities for improvement. Constant improvement in all aspects of a company's operation can give a company the edge it needs to stay competitive in today's global marketplace.

To evaluate effectiveness and identify opportunities for improvement, an auditor must look at the merit of the procedures. A procedure has merit to the extent that it fulfills the company's needs, accomplishes its stated purpose, and contributes to making the quality policy more than just words on a plaque. That is to say, it must contribute to fulfilling the goals of the quality policy.

Audits are not limited to scheduled, formal evaluations of procedure compliance. Audits can be done to help solve a problem, verify quality, or monitor the manufacturing process. Auditing can indicate where a procedure went wrong, or if a noncompliance caused the defect. It can identify when a problem first showed up, or where to best implement corrective action. There is nothing wrong with doing specialized, unscheduled audits, as long as they are included in written procedures for internal auditing.

CHAPTER 2

Who Is Audited

Remember that the system and not the people are being audited. The system comprises procedures that are carried out by people who perform the appropriate job functions. When auditing, the word "who" really refers to which job function. It does not refer to the identity of an individual.

Whoever Follows Your Procedures

The question of who to audit can be answered by saying anyone who follows your procedures should be audited. That is to say, whoever carries out the quality system. And that would entail the majority of the job functions in the company! However, depending on the size of the company, auditing everyone who carries out the system is most likely to be an impossible task.

When a few pertinent facts are considered, the task of identifying which job functions to audit is scaled down considerably. The task of auditing is often made more manageable by having a team of auditors audit more than one section simultaneously. Alternatively, only a specific function or section of the whole system can be audited. Various sections may be audited separately, one at a time, according to a schedule that may take a year to complete. Typically, the schedule is such that only one or two parts of the system are audited a month. So during any one particular audit a rather small part of the whole system is being audited.

Essentially, every company needs at least two auditors who work in different departments. Three to six auditors per one hundred people is common. They must not report to the same person. Good auditing practice forbids anyone to audit himself, his supervisor, or the activities and job functions within his own department. In a small company none of the auditors should be in the same department. In a large company virtually every department should be represented on the auditing staff. Whoever schedules which auditors will audit what and when has the responsibility to make sure that no one audits his own job function, his supervisor, or anyone else in his department.

Only one department performs some parts of the quality system. The number of people in that department will be more or less proportional to the volume of work. The records examined should be a representative sample of all the work accomplished since the last audit. This sample size should be proportionate to the volume of work done. The number of people who are spoken to will correspond to this sample size. If possible, different items should be sampled and different people should be spoken to each time that particular audit is done.

For example, let's say inspection and testing is being audited. The inspection supervisor, of course, will have to be spoken to. Also in the audit, observe inspectors to see that they are following the prescribed instructions. If there are nine inspectors, the audit may choose to observe only two of them, but not the same two who were chosen the last time this audit was done. Thus, out of a department of 10 people, three people were observed — the supervisor and two inspectors. The auditor will want to see some more inspection records to verify that the inspection system is routinely being followed. Three more inspection records may be looked at, but not the same three that were examined the last time. This would be a reasonable sampling of the activities in that department. If design control were being audited, the auditor would have met with the engineering manager and a proportionate number of engineers, depending on the size of the engineering department.

Managers and Supervisors

In the examples mentioned previously, both times the auditor would have talked to the person in charge. That should be the starting point. If the person in charge does any part of the procedure himself, the auditor needs to be satisfied that he knows and uses his part of the procedure. It may be that subordinates do the entire procedure. Even then, the supervisor would be the one making the determination of who in the department is actually carrying out the procedure. The person in charge would know who and where the person is located. The supervisor may even schedule a time for the auditor to meet the subordinate. Therefore, it is the supervisor or manager who connects the auditor to the right person. The supervisor can also tell the auditor how many people are carrying out that procedure and the size of the workload so the auditor can determine how many people to talk to and the sample size of the audit.

Set the tone of the audit with the head of the department. Never be adversarial. The auditor needs the manager's cooperation to do the audit properly. An audit is an intrusion on the everyday routine of that department, so schedule the time for the audit and personnel needed with the department head's agreement. Do not forget to thank the manager at the end of the audit.

When the auditor is finished examining the evidence, the findings should be reviewed with the responsible manager. Ultimately, the manager is responsible for making sure the procedures are properly followed in his department. The auditor should also discuss corrective action with the manager, since he is providing the time, money, personnel, and other resources to implement the corrective actions.

Non-management Personnel

A quality system is composed of a group of procedures that describe the activities that must be carried out to achieve the goals of the company's quality policy. In some cases this is a management process carried out by a manager. In other cases a subordinate (e.g., direct labor) carries it out. If, after meeting with the responsible manager, it is determined that the procedure is carried out by a subordinate or group of subordinates, ask to speak with the subordinates.

The auditor will want to talk with those who carry out the activities on a day-to-day basis. The auditor will want to talk to them, rather than talking only to a supervisor or manager, because they are usually more intimately involved with the process than a manager or supervisor would be. They know the shortcomings of the process as well as its strong points. They know the amount of time and effort it requires, rather than some theoretical or mathematical amount that the manager may use for planning purposes.

If the company has a labor union, the auditor should be familiar with any applicable policies or any contract provisions that may apply. In some cases a shop steward may have to be present during questioning. It all depends on the situation at that particular company.

The People Who Carry Out the Process

The people performing the process may be in-house contractors, temporary employees, company employees borrowed from another department, or regular employees who do it everyday. For auditing purposes they are all treated the same. Ask them to explain what they are doing and how they do it. Observe what they do. Ask questions about hypothetical situations. No one knows more about who does what, where, when, and how, than the people who do it. They are a great resource for an auditor. Employees who work in a specific department every day know the strong and weak points of that department. Therefore, they can help you assess the effectiveness of a procedure.

Every audit requires the examination of evidence. This evidence may take the form of material, parts, photographs, written records, computer files, etc. Any record required by the procedure is evidence that the process was done. Talk to the people who made the parts, took the photographs, or filled out the forms. Question them about what they did and compare it to the written procedure. Artifacts can also be considered evidence. If the procedure says to paint something orange and orange paint is seen splattered about here and there, that is evidence. If all that is seen is a little blue paint splatter, then ask the person holding the paint sprayer about it.

Deliberately not following a procedure may indicate that the procedure does not meet the employee's needs. That is to say, it is not an effective procedure. Question the employee on the reasons for altering the procedure, without accusing him of a violation. The employee will speak to the auditor more openly and less defensively if it is not mentioned that the procedure is different from what he is doing. Find out if his way is better. Determine if any need is being met that would not be met if the procedure were followed exactly. When the employee follows the process as specified, he may be doing so out of discipline or trust in the system. However, he may have ideas about how it may be done better. An auditor should look for opportunities to improve the process. The people who carry out the process may already know some.

CHAPTER 3

What to Audit

When conducting quality audits, the auditor is auditing the system and processes; the system is a group of related procedures (in ISO 9000 and QS-9000 systems they are called elements) that when carried out, achieve the goals stated in the quality policy. A procedure is audited, when scheduled, by verifying compliance to the written procedure. Thus the auditor is checking to see if who does what, when, where, and how, is the same as prescribed in the documentation. The auditor is also checking the effectiveness of how they meet the requirements of each element, and looking for opportunities for improvement.

The 20 Elements of ISO 9001

ISO 9001 has 20 elements, each covering a different aspect of a complete quality management system. All 20 elements need to be audited according to a schedule. The schedule is usually annual, so every element is audited at least once a year. ISO 9001 requires a company to schedule the audits on the basis of status and importance of the activity being audited. Therefore, elements of high importance or certain status are scheduled for more frequent audits.

These elements cover all aspects of the quality system. They include management responsibilities, design control, process control, inspection and test status, nonconformances, etc. For a complete listing and description, see the ISO 9000 standard itself. ANSI/ASQ 9001 and QS-9000 also include the ISO requirements in their entirety. QS-9000, which was developed for the automotive industry, includes the sector specific sections that must be audited as well. QS-9000 contains the full text of the ISO 9000 requirements, plus the customer-specific requirements of the automotive industry.

It is up to each company to determine the audit frequency of each element. Many companies audit the entire system only once for the first year, then they adjust the audit schedule according to the first-year audit results. This author suggests auditing elements 4.5, Document and Data Control, and 4.9, Process Control, more frequently, since many companies find they have a higher incidence of noncompliance.

Non-ISO 9000 Systems

There are other quality system requirements that are not ISO 9000 related. There are even many quality systems that have been put in place to meet company needs without intending to meet any specific quality system standard at all. Regardless of the system that is being audited, there are certain items to address regarding the scope of an audit. For the particular topic, function, department, procedure, etc. to be audited, obtain the following and use them to determine what the audit must cover:

- All applicable policies, procedures, forms, and instructions.
- Appointment with and name of the supervisor or manager with whom to start.
- Approximate number of people performing the task.
- Applicable safety gear (hearing protection, safety glasses, etc.).
- Previous audit reports and corrective actions.

The auditor may also want to determine the proportion of factory space or other company resources devoted to the audit topic. Once this information is known, review it thoroughly and determine the scope of the audit. The scope is all the aspects of the element that the auditor intends to cover in the amount of time and factory space the auditor intends to use to cover it. In some companies the person in charge of all auditing, often called an audit program manager, lead auditor, or auditor supervisor, determines the scope regardless of who performs the audit. In other cases the scope is left to the discretion of the auditors.

If a flowchart of the procedure exists in the official documentation, the auditor should get a copy and use it as a guide in auditing. If an official one does not exist, constructing one while auditing may help to understand the procedure or the process. Every audit of every element should explore who does what, when, where, and how. When something does not make sense, or is not mentioned in the documentation, then ask why. These questions can be asked of all system elements.

Processes

In addition to the procedures developed for the system, most likely there are individual work instructions that describe how to do each task. When auditing, verify that these operations are correctly being performed. The auditor is not limited to the scheduled audits of the whole procedure. Nothing prevents the auditor from conducting additional audits of the manufacturing operations to see if they are being properly performed, as long as the auditing procedures note that the auditor is going to perform unscheduled audits *in addition* to the regular scheduled audits of process control. Such audits are a useful problem prevention tool.

The auditor can review documents like process sheets, shop routing sheets, work instructions, and the like on a monthly basis to verify proper processing. He can watch work in process, observe operations, review records, etc. on a regular basis if he likes. If one company has 12 assembly lines, each one should be audited during a different month. This is to verify work in process is done per all work instructions.

Product

Auditing of product is usually done during a dock audit. Typically a dock audit happens like this: The auditor obtains a list of all customer complaints in the last six months. Then they unpackage a sample of the shipment just before it is shipped and verify that all the product in the sample do not exhibit any of the customer complaints. Then the sample is repackaged. The auditor witnesses the repackaging. After repackaging, all of the appropriate shipping documents are reviewed for accuracy and completeness by the auditor. Finally, the correct destination is verified. This completes the dock audit.

Auditing of product quality is not limited to dock audits. Another type of product audit is a stockroom or warehouse check. This is when the auditor checks the handling, storage, and FIFO (First In First Out) rotation of the parts as they sit in the stockroom or warehouse. Such parts audits are actually a frequent monitoring of some aspects of element 4.15, which include handling, storage, packaging, preservation and delivery, while other activities of this requirement are checked during the scheduled audit of this element.

Nothing prevents the auditor from monitoring the work in process this way by doing several small periodic, unscheduled, often monthly audits as long as system procedures and instructions say the audits will be done. They are best done in addition to the regularly scheduled audits. They often allow the identification of small problems before they become major customer concerns.

Service Activities

If a company has a service department that repairs or replaces customer returns, do not neglect this area. If it exists, then it must be in the audit schedule. The process and parts (product) audits in this department can be done in a way similar to the audits done in the production stage. Audit using the service process sheets, routing sheets, etc. that the company uses.

If on-site servicing is available at the customer's location, the auditor may audit this also. Nothing in the ISO 9001 standards forbids an audit of on-site service. Whether or not the auditor should do this depends on the company's relationship with its customers, its available resources, and its own internal auditing procedure.

CHAPTER 4

Where to Conduct Audits

While a conference room can provide a convenient and somewhat private place to conduct an audit interview or to review records, it is not a good place to conduct audits. The people performing the processes the auditor is auditing do not know exactly what the auditor is going to ask or which evidence the auditor wants to see. Consequently, the auditor will often have to wait while they leave to find someone or get something. Auditees can more easily show the procedure where it is actually performed. Records will be more easily and quickly obtained as well.

If the auditor reviews only the records they brought with them, then the auditor is seeing only what they chose to show him. Explanations they give will be only what they choose to tell the auditor and may be harder to follow. The auditor will not be able to judge the lighting or orderliness of the area in which the procedure is done. He will not be able to see how the procedures relate to each other in the system and be less able to judge their effectiveness. It is better for the auditor to go to where the procedure is carried out and conduct the audit there.

Where the Activity Takes Place

If an auditor goes to where the activity takes place, he will observe more than he could with mere explanations. The auditor will also have more insight into what to ask. A demonstration of the procedure can tell an auditor much more than a mere explanation.

Where a procedure takes place is often not prescribed. This is because most procedures take place either in locations that are obvious or in multiple, sometimes indefinite (unspecified) locations. Different parts of a procedure may be done in different places. Some aspects may be done in a supervisor or manager's office; others may be done on the shop floor. Records may be kept in a manager's office or in a designated file cabinet located elsewhere. In any case, the responsible manager or supervisor should know what takes place, where, when, and where the records are kept.

Responsible Manager's Office

Some functions of the quality system are performed entirely by management. These include but are not limited to management reviews, contract reviews, engineering changes, and purchasing. Others, such as disposition of nonconforming product and employee training, are partially done by management or supervisory personnel. The office of the management-level person responsible for performance of an element is a good place to start. This person can show the auditor whatever his part in the procedure is. All appropriate records may be in his office or else he will know where to get them. A supervisor can answer whatever questions the auditor asks that pertain to him. If an auditor asks something that the supervisor cannot answer, he can direct the auditor to the person who can. If the supervisor does not have a particular record, he can obtain it from the person who does. The responsible manager's office is always a good starting point. For a few elements, it is the only place the auditor needs to go. However, the auditor should not hesitate to go to another location, even if it is to another person's office. The auditor should access what is really going on.

On the Shop Floor

If the entire procedure is not done in an office environment (and most are not), then the auditor should go to the place where it is done. Often this will be the shop floor. It could be a production area, a warehouse floor, or a department set aside for production. Where the auditor really wants to go is wherever the procedure is actually performed. This is often, but not necessarily, the room or floor area where the applicable department does its work. If auditing calibration, this might be a calibration lab, a metrology department, a quality department, or even a tool crib.

After auditing in the place where it happens, the auditc should go to where the results are applied. If auditing calibration, this would be an inspection area where the gauges are actually used or a tool room or production area where raw material is measured while being worked on. Include in the audit anywhere that work in process is checked. In these locations, check if the measurement devices are in calibration and that they are used and stored as specified.

If auditing handling, storage, packaging, preservation, and delivery, after talking to the supervisor and listening to explanations by a worker, the auditor should go to the warehouse or stock room and observe handling and storage practices. The auditor should go to where the product is packaged and watch it happen. The auditor should also observe shipping and receiving in progress on location. While making these observations, the auditor should not hesitate to ask questions. The auditor should compare what he sees with what is prescribed in the documentation.

CHAPTER 5

When to Conduct Audits

Audits should be scheduled on the basis of the status (e.g., past performance, customer complaints, etc.) and importance of the activity being audited. While this gives each company wide latitudes as to how and when it wants to schedule the audits, it does require consideration of the status and importance of each activity. Therefore, not all elements of the system need to be audited with the same frequency. Furthermore, the audits do not need to be evenly spaced throughout the year. The audit schedule has to reflect the strengths and weaknesses of the quality system, the volume of work performed in the various departments, company schedules, and the unique characteristics of a particular company.

Here are three examples of how to schedule audits:

1. If the raw materials are available only seasonally, then the audit of purchasing should only be done during the season in which the materials are bought.
2. If most customer complaints were about packaging, preservation, and delivery, then these areas would be audited more often.
3. If the company has been auditing control of customer supplied product twice a year, and a three-year audit history shows there has never been a noncompliance, then the company may consider auditing that element only once a year.

ISO 9000 standards for quality systems do not specifically say what characteristics of status an activity has to have in order to warrant more or less frequent audits—that is left to the company. Here are some principles to follow when deciding how frequently to audit an activity. These are rules of thumb, not commandments.

1. An activity that has a history of noncompliance from previous audits should be audited more frequently.
2. Any activity that has a reputation of poor quality should also be audited more frequently.
3. Do additional audits on an activity if it has a very high turnover of personnel.
4. Audit an activity when it is first started up if it is performed very infrequently.
5. Seasonal activities should be audited during the applicable season or immediately after they occur.

6. Audit frequencies can be changed according to audit history or to accommodate changes within the company.

Other factors to consider when scheduling audits are existing workloads, new programs, and contract requirements. Fast-paced work or heavy workloads provide motivation to create shortcuts and may even alter the effectiveness of the procedures. New programs are prone to noncompliance because workers are not as familiar with the procedures. Some contracts may have their own auditing requirements. Consider these factors when creating the audit schedule and determining audit frequency.

Scheduled and Unscheduled Audits

The audits that are required by ISO 9000 standards need to be scheduled. This schedule must be documented and is usually incorporated into an audit procedure or instruction of some kind. There is nothing secret about the audit schedule. It may be posted on a bulletin board. This is contrary to some people's way of thinking. They believe that the company should not know ahead of time that it is going to be audited. This is so the company can be caught not complying with procedures. If a department or work group is deliberately not complying with procedures, the department already knows it, so catching it in the act contributes nothing new. If the department's noncompliance is not deliberate, then whether or not it knows the auditor is coming makes no difference because the department is not trying to hide anything.

This is not to say that unscheduled audits should never be done. A company functions on many interrelated activities and sometimes the unexpected happens. Personnel changes may cause a sudden change in the effectiveness of a procedure. Quality problems may suddenly occur. Any number of events may happen that do not lend themselves to the audit schedule. There are times when an unscheduled audit should be done. Such audits are usually to help solve or even prevent problems rather than merely verify compliance. Here are three examples:

1. If a very important customer returns a large quantity of product for a particular defect, an audit of process control may indicate why it was not caught during production or even where in the production process to control it. In a case like this, an audit should be done right away to help address the problem rather than waiting several months to do it per the schedule. The regularly scheduled process control audit can still be done per the schedule.

2. A department is developing a backlog of work. It could be a normal increase in workload. However, it could also mean that a procedure is no longer as effective as it should be. An unscheduled audit of that procedure is justified since one purpose of conducting an audit is to determine the effectiveness of a procedure.

3. Management reviews some audit results and determines that a particular element should be audited twice a year instead of once a year. The auditor may

want to start the second audit right away, depending on how long ago the last audit was done.

Investigative Audits

Investigative audits are conducted to look for something in particular. They may investigate a procedure in depth to find out what can be the root cause of a problem or to verify an already suspected root cause. A word of caution here: An audit is not a witch hunt. Audits are not done in order to assign blame or identify a scapegoat. The audit is only a tool to help solve a problem. An audit's help is limited to verifying compliance, checking effectiveness, and identifying opportunities for improvement. Any other use of auditing will destroy people's perspectives on auditing and create adversarial attitudes and behaviors. Audits can either improve a corporate culture or ruin it.

CHAPTER 6

How to Conduct an Audit

Most companies use either one of three common approaches to auditing: 1. The company has a list of predetermined questions. 2. The auditors develop their own questions. 3. The company has a list of questions and gives the auditors the freedom to probe more at their discretion. The approach used depends mostly on the kind of audit being done, its purpose, and the level of training of the auditors.

When auditing an entire system in one audit a questionnaire is often used. It is a checklist of predetermined questions, which may be asked in yes or no fashion. This kind of audit is like an attribute inspection and is pass or fail. The company meets requirements or does not meet requirements. The questions are on an audit form and the same form is always used for the same audit. If auditing a process, then each process will usually have its own audit checklist.

This attribute type of audit can be used when evaluating a supplier. One list of questions can be applied to all suppliers. Alternatively, there can be different checklists for different kinds of suppliers, e.g., a metal-plating company will have a different checklist from a metal-casting supplier. Such an audit is used to determine if a supplier can or cannot meet certain requirements. This type of audit may also be applied to a process or procedure to verify if the procedure is, or is not, meeting certain requirements. Such audits have several advantages:

- They are easy to do.
- They take less time.
- They require only minimal auditor training and auditing skill.
- The quality and depth of the audits are consistent.

They also tell the auditor less about the subject being audited. To address this issue, there is often a place for auditor comments. Since people with varying degrees of auditor training do audits of this type, the observations and comments are of variable value. Rarely do the questionnaires allow for additional questions from the auditor. Still, if consistent quality of audits is a major concern and auditor training is minimal, this may be the reasonable choice.

The questions are developed by first researching the needs and requirements that are applicable. Then each requirement/need should be listed separately in a logical order. The auditor should form a yes or no question about each one. It may be phrased as, "do you have ..." or "is there used...," even "can you ..." or "are there...". This should be done for each requirement or procedure step. If there are too many questions, the auditor can prioritize the requirements first and form questions from only those that are of sufficient priority. Figure 6-1 is a sample attribute type audit checklist for auditing element 4.9, Process Control of an ISO 9000 System. This is only an example and is not intended to be all-inclusive.

The second common approach to auditing is when the auditors develop their own questions after familiarizing themselves with the written documentation. Indeed, they may use the written documents to help them develop the audit questions. The questions should be developed before the audit begins.

Although rarely used for supplier evaluation in the past, some believe this approach is becoming more common for supplier audits. It is most frequently used to audit specific sections of a quality system. The best use for this approach is with audits performed to find the root cause of a problem, since nothing limits how deeply the auditor probes. It is not only the best approach for problem-solving audits, it is also best for identifying areas that need improvement.

These are the steps that an auditor should follow when developing the questions for this approach to auditing. First, study the applicable policies and procedures. The policies will tell the auditor about the attitude and philosophy that the company is attempting to use. The procedures will tell the auditor who does what and when. Next, for *every* step in the procedure the auditor should ask who does it, what is done, when is it done, where is it done, how is it done, what evidence is there that it was done, etc. When conducting the audit, the auditor should observe the procedure being done,

Figure 6-1. Sample Attribute Audit Checklist for Process Control

Audit Type	Internal	Supplier	Other(explian)	Date
Topic/Scope of Audit: Process Control				
Location of Audit:				
Responsible Manager for Audit Area:				
Other Contacts:				
Auditor(s):				

Question	Compliance	
	Yes	No
1. Does the supplier have written procedures for production, installation, and servicing as applicable to processing?		
2. Does the supplier have a suitable working environment for the processes being carried out?		
3. Does the supplier have all necessary equipment, gauges, personnel, and facilities to control the process?		
4. Are applicable standards, specifications, and engineering drawings available to the appropriate people?		
5. Are the process inputs (raw material, sub assemblies, parts, etc.) properly identified and monitored?		
6. Is there in-process monitoring of the process that is capable of detecting a loss in process capability?		
7. Is the process output monitored and checked against the applicable requirements?		
8. Is the process monitored by the supplier's personnel with the knowledge and authority to adjust the process?		
9. Does the supplier have customer approval for the processes as required?		
10. Is there a system in place and being used that assures proper maintenance of the equipment that would affect product quality?		

when practical, and ask for evidence that each step in the procedure is being followed.

When conducting the audit the auditor may have to rephrase or explain some of the questions in order to communicate most effectively with the company. This is normal. The auditor should take sufficient notes to refresh his memory. The auditor should not transcribe the conversation. Note taking should be used as a memory jogging tool and not as the audit record.

After the audit interview, the auditor should compare the answers to the questions, the evidence that was gathered, and the activities that were witnessed with the documentation. The auditor should try to reconcile any differences by asking more questions and probing for more information. Any difference between the documentation and the evidence, explanations, or activities is a possible noncompliance. After the questions have all been asked and the auditor has had a chance to learn who does what, when, where, and how, the auditor should talk with the company about opportunities for improvement. Is there a better way? "Better" could mean more efficient, less time consuming, less costly, less paperwork, etc. The auditor should then discuss any possible noncompliance with the responsible manager. If problems to the documentation cannot be reconciled to the auditor's satisfaction, then they are a noncompliance. If there are no differences, or the differences are reconciled in a second interview, then there is no noncompliance.

The auditor should then write the audit report. This should consist of a summary narrative of the audit along with any noncompliance. It should also include the auditor's observations as well as any concerns that are not a noncompliance but could eventually lead to or cause one. The auditor should also identify any areas of improvement.

As illustrated, this approach to auditing is more difficult. It requires more preparation and takes longer to do, but there are some advantages.

- It covers more of the procedure, i.e., the audits have more depth.
- It is easier to identify areas of improvement.
- The audit records provide more information.

When used for internal auditing by one person, it is usually done on only one system element or procedure at a time. This is one reason for auditing different parts of the whole system throughout the year. However, a team approach works well also. Figure 6-2 is an example of this type of audit question sheet for element 4.6, Purchasing in an ISO 9000 System. Again, this is only an example and is not intended to be all-inclusive. In the appendix there is a form that may be used when auditing this way.

Combined Approach

While either one of these approaches can be done by itself, there has been great success in combining them. This third approach to auditing is done by keeping the questions on the checklist more general. The auditors use the checklist as a starting point and have the freedom to pursue avenues of questioning at their own discretion. This can help an auditor find which audit trail to follow or identify where and when to probe more deeply. Sometimes there may be very few ques-

Figure 6-2. Sample Audit Questions for Audit of Purchasing

Audit Type	Internal	Supplier	Other (explain)	Date
Topic/Scope of Audit: Purchasing				
Location of Audit:				
Responsible Manager for Audit Area:				
Other Contacts:				
Auditor(s):				

Question		Compliance
1. What procedures do you have that ensure purchased products and services meet the applicable requirements?		
2. How are your suppliers selected?		
3. How do you evaluate a supplier's ability to meet all the requirements?		
4. What controls do you apply to your suppliers to assure a satisfactory level of quality?		
5. What records do you keep to verify that suppliers provide acceptable products or services?		
6. What descriptive and technical information is on your purchase orders?		
7. How do customer and internal quality requirements get put on your purchase orders?		

tions predetermined and the auditor may ask many others in order to probe further. A combination of standard questions and auditor freedom to pursue questions at his discretion is the usual approach to ISO or QS 9000 certification and surveillance audits.

The company should consider the time and resources available, the purposes of the audit, the auditor's level of training, and the advantages disadvantages of each approach. The company should then decide which approach to auditing best meets its needs. This combined approach can also be done using audit teams.

Team Auditing

In large companies it may take several auditors working several days to complete the audit of an entire system. However, internal audits of part of the system may also be conducted in teams. If the members of an auditing team are chosen from different departments and different levels of management, then each team member will bring a different perspective to the topic being audited. Each team member can contribute a different slant to the audit questions when they are being developed. The input from different perspectives allows for much more comprehensive and well-rounded questions. Additionally, such audit team members can much more easily find opportunities for improvement. If the department from which an audit team member comes is an internal customer or internal supplier to the auditee, the team may have insight into which specific areas need to be examined more closely.

When choosing audit team members, care must be taken that they are all neutral to the auditee. They must not work for the auditee nor have the auditee report to them. They must not work in the same department nor have financial interest in the audit outcome.

Audit teams typically comprise from two to five people. One of these people is chosen as the team leader. It is often the team that makes this choice. The team leader acts as a coordinator. He or she sets the dates for team meetings, makes the appointments for the audit interviews, and keeps the team focused and on track.

All of the team members work on developing all of the questions. This maximizes the effect of the various perspectives and should be done even if the team is going to split up and interview different people.

Sometimes the entire team will meet with one auditee. Sometimes the team may split up and talk with different people working in the same function. For example, a team of four auditors is auditing the inspection and test function. After they have developed their questions, the questions can be categorized into receiving inspection, in-process inspection, final inspection, and other inspection questions relating to planning, training, inspection staffing, inspection department housekeeping, etc. The team then splits up, one auditor talks with a receiving inspector, one with an in-process inspector, one with a final inspector, and one with the inspection supervisor. Afterward the team members discuss the results among themselves. Then they have a closing meeting with all of the people they interviewed.

This is only one way a team audit may be done. Another way is for the whole team to meet as a group with each person. Another way is for the whole audit team to meet with the supervisor and chosen inspectors all at once. The teams usually decide how they want to do it, although some companies may have specific policies or procedures on how it is to be done.

Topic and Scope of the Audit

Some companies will audit different sections of their quality system according to a schedule. The schedule is designed so that the entire system is covered once a year. Other companies use schedules that cover the system two or three times a year. These companies are usually trying to use auditing as a police-like method to get people to follow their written procedures. Actually, not following procedures is more likely a symptom for either poor procedures or a lack of total commitment to the system. More frequent auditing will not solve these problems. Such frequent auditing often lacks depth and is not identifying the real problems. ISO 9000 and QS 9000 audits are usually done element by element with a complete audit schedule covering all 20 elements (23 in QS 9000). Often the audit schedule identifies which elements shall be audited during which months. While this is a common practice, it is not the only way to choose what topic to audit.

Some companies group the elements into functions. For example, purchasing, customer furnished material, packaging preservation and handling, and traceability can all be considered part of the materials-management function and be audited together as a materials-management function. Inspection and testing, inspection status, gauge control and calibration, and nonconforming material can all be grouped into an audit of the inspection function. This is a perfectly acceptable way of determining and scheduling the audit topics as long as some type of audit covers every part of the system.

The scope of an audit can be thought of as how much of the audit topic the company is going to cover or how deep the auditor is going to go. The auditor or audit team may decide or the individual who has overall responsibility for auditing within the company can determine the scope. If the audit has been requested then the person who made the request can determine the scope. If the audit is being done to investigate a problem then the scope can be limited by the nature of the investigation or the person responsible for solving the problem.

Too broad a scope can make an audit too expensive, too time consuming, or overly intrusive. Any one of these is poor auditing practice and hinders the cooperation between the auditor and the company. Too narrow a scope risks missing opportunities for improvement, not solving a problem, or missing a noncompliance. Any of these is a poor audit result and can make everyone regard the audits as useless.

Audit Scoring

In attribute-style audits, the audit is usually scored by calculating the percent of questions that have an acceptable answer. If some questions are deemed more important or more complex than others are, then those questions can be weighted. In this case, the audit can be scored by adding the total weights of the acceptable answers and calculating that as a percent of the total possible weight of all questions. In either case the audit "passes" or "fails" according to whether or not the score meets a predetermined minimum value.

When audit questions are open-ended (not yes/no questions), various score values are assigned to each question as it is answered during the audit. This is based on the auditor's assessment of the merit of the answer. The audit score is the total of all answer scores. Here again, "pass" or "fail" depends on meeting a certain predetermined minimum number of points. This requires greater auditor skill and judgment to assign the point values fairly, accurately, and consistently to the answers received.

Recently, with the increase in the number of companies becoming ISO 9000 registered, the classification of noncompliance as major or minor has come into more use. A company usually "fails" an audit if there is a major noncompliance found. A few minor noncompliances, typically two or three, are acceptable if there is a commitment to do corrective action. More than a couple of minor noncompliances are usually considered a major noncompliance.

Whatever method of scoring an audit is used should be described in the company's internal audit procedures.

CHAPTER 7

Audit Reports

An audit report is more than just an historical record of the audit. It is a marker by which progress is measured and a tool to help management steer the company. It is a prompt that tells the follow-up auditor what corrective actions to verify. It is a communications tool that explains the results of the audit to the manager responsible for the area that was audited. The audit reports are also used as an important part of management-review activities since they contain valuable information on the status of the system as well as company operations. As objective records of what is really happening throughout the company, audit reports are valuable input to management in decision-making, planning, guidance, and other management activities. Once the entire system has been audited, the audit reports can be analyzed to find the weak spots in the quality system and even find patterns of behavior within the corporate culture that may be adversely affecting quality.

An audit report is both evidence that the audit procedure was done and a record of the information learned during the audit. Since the report is itself a record, it is therefore subject to an audit during any audit of quality records. It must be maintained like any other record. However, it is not a record to be placed in a file and forgotten. It must be *used*.

Audit reports also provide auditors with guidance on the scope and topics to cover in future audits. The same auditors should not be auditing the same elements with the same questions all the time. Reviewing a previous audit report for the element can provide information on strengths and weaknesses, which records to review, who to talk with, and other information as well. An auditor would normally not want to repeat the exact questions as the previous audit because they would tell the auditor nothing new. Likewise, if the same function were performed by a group of people, the auditor would not talk to the same individual all the time. Some companies deliberately have different auditors do an element each time that element is audited. This makes the audit record a valuable guide for auditors. The amount of time audit reports are kept must be specified in the quality system. Three years is common, but keeping the records seven or 10 years is not unreasonable.

Content

The content of the audit report will depend on the audit approach used. If a predetermined checklist is used then the audit report is a brief narrative summary of the audit including the auditor's comments and a copy of the completed checklist. If the auditor asked the questions and had the freedom to pursue an audit trail then the report is a more detailed summary. This would include the information learned from the interview, observations and concerns, and any identified areas of improvement. Regardless of which approach to auditing is used, the audit report must also include the noncompliance reports with their evidence as well as evidence of compliance gathered during the audit.

Included with every audit report is any noncompliance identified during the audit. These may be violations of written policies, procedures, or instructions. If the quality system is supposed to meet the requirements of a published, recognized standard like ISO 9000 or QS 9000, then any violation of these system requirements is also a noncompliance. Undocumented procedures, if they are quality activities, are noncompliances. Violations of the quality policy can also be noncompliance. Any of these, if they occur, must be recorded on the appropriate form and are a permanent part of the audit record. Any corrective action generated by them is also part of the audit record. A sample noncompliance report can be found in the appendix.

When audits are scored, the score should be recorded on the audit report. There may be a minimum-passing grade that requires corrective action if not met. Pass/fail status, as well as the passing criteria, should also be on the report. When a corrective action is called for, this fact should be in the audit record, usually on the noncompliance form. Expected dates of corrective action completion and date of planned follow-up audits should also be indicated. Not all audits are scored. When noncompliances are classified as minor, major, or critical, passing the audit usually means having no critical or majors and only a limited number of minors, typically a maximum of two or three.

Noncompliance

The term noncompliance is used rather than nonconformance in order to distinguish the fact that they apply to a defect in the system or procedure, rather than a defect in a physical part. Hence the procedure, as carried out by the people, does not comply with the written requirements. The following are examples of some types of noncompliance found in audits:

- The policy, procedure, or instruction is not documented.
- A form used is not referenced anywhere in the system.
- The procedure contradicts or does not support the applicable policy.
- The procedure or instructions are not being followed.
- The requirements of an applicable standard are not being fulfilled.
- Evidence of proper fulfillment of a procedure or instruction is lacking or incomplete.

Noncompliances are often classified as "major" or "minor." Some companies have an additional classification like "critical." Generally speaking, a major noncompliance has serious results and is caused by a complete breakdown of part of the system or the total absence of a required procedure. Companies that have a "critical" category may consider a noncompliance critical if it could have catastrophic results.

Minor noncompliances are less severe in nature, often resulting from only a partial breakdown of a single procedure or instruction, or incomplete evidence. They may grow into a major noncompliance if left alone. Therefore, it is still important to have them corrected.

Some companies allow the auditor to include "concerns" in an audit report. These are not noncompliances. They are items that have the potential to become noncompliances. Taking action on them before they become problems is a sound quality practice to be encouraged. However, care must be exercised so as to not become over zealous in identifying and correcting problems that do not yet, and may not ever, exist.

In some cases, auditors may include "observations." These are neither concerns nor noncompliances. They are really reminder notes that an auditor puts into an audit report as a memory aid for future audits. They may remind an auditor that a particular audit trail does not need to be pursued or they can remind an auditor to pursue a particular audit trail. The may also notify future auditors of unusual or unexpected (but still acceptable) facts. In any case, observations and concerns do not require corrective actions, whereas noncompliance, whether critical, major, or minor, do require correction.

Distribution

If the audit was done by a team of auditors, they should all review and agree on the content of the report. The auditee or the responsible manager should see a draft copy of the report before it gets distributed to anyone else. If several people were audited as a group, they can be assembled in a conference room. The draft copy of the audit report should be discussed with the auditees, as their input is valuable. Such a meeting to discuss the audit report is important to resolve any misunderstandings or miscommunications, determine reasonable corrective action completion dates, and schedule any follow-up audit that may be necessary. As a result of this meeting a final copy of the audit report is written and distributed. A company's internal audit procedure tells the auditor who receives copies of the internal audits. The responsible manager and the quality department manager should each get one, as they are the two people most responsible for making sure that any noncompliance is resolved. They also have a vested interest in areas of improvement.

Many companies keep audit reports confidential because they may contain information that competitors may use to their advantage. However, a distribution policy that is too restrictive can also hurt the company. Obviously the responsible managers need to know the results, but others may have insight as to how to best resolve issues. Furthermore, very few of the sections of a complete system are performed by just one department. Many activities are multi-disciplinary and therefore several departments should be involved in developing solutions. Managers from these other departments should see the results of the audit. It is not a good idea for only managers to see audit results.

The people who were actually carrying out the procedure while it was being audited need to know the results and need to know what the auditor was looking for. It is a real advantage for them to see the audit reports.

CHAPTER 8

Corrective Actions

When an audit calls for corrective action it is because the auditor has found a noncompliance. Such a noncompliance could exist because a part of the quality system is lacking or a procedure is only partially implemented, not being followed, or lacking evidence. When audit answers are scored with a numerical value, corrective action may be required if the score is too low.

In the case of a yes/no-type checklist audit, it is usually because the system or procedure was either lacking something or was not being followed correctly. Corrective actions in this situation are often a matter of revising the system to include what it lacks, training personnel, or revising the procedure to make it more error-resistant.

If the audit is scored and fails due to a low score, corrective action is a matter of revising the policies, procedures, and instructions to upgrade the answers with low scores. Training and better record keeping are also prudent if the score was due to lack of or poor evidence.

Corrective actions must be documented and are a part of the audit record. They must be kept on file for the prescribed length of time. Copies of the corrective-action statements can provide valuable information to inspectors and auditors. In fact, auditors should always review completed corrective actions applicable to the topic being audited as part of preparation for doing the audit.

The auditor and auditee should also agree on when the corrective action is to be implemented. The auditee fills out a form describing the corrective action. It is usually the same form on which the noncompliance is described, but may be a separate form. The level of detail included in the corrective-action description varies but should include the following:

- Who is responsible for implementing the corrective action,
- Root cause of the noncompliance,
- Description of the action itself, including any changes it requires to be made,
- Date and location in which corrective action will be implemented, and
- Description of the means by which the effectiveness of the action will be verified.

Sometimes corrective actions may need to be more developed, depending on the problem. When the noncompliance was found in the type of audit where the auditor developed his own questions and was free to probe more deeply, more research may have to be done to find the root cause and develop the corrective action. A full-blown corrective-action development may be necessary using many of the classic tools of TQM, or disciplined methods, including but not limited to, fishbone diagrams, Pareto charts, statistics, etc. It all depends on the nature of the noncompliance. Related noncompliance may have similar or even identical causes. Occasionally, one corrective action may apply to more than one noncompliance if well thought out and complete enough. However, one corrective action answering more than one noncompliance is a rarity. Most often, an audit report that has more than one noncompliance will require more than one corrective action.

Corrective actions should be implemented as soon as possible after the audit—two or three weeks are common. Four weeks are still reasonable. Five weeks begin to seem like procrastination. If there is a legitimate reason for a corrective action to take more than that, then the reason should be documented in the audit report. This should be a rarity.

Implementation of the corrective action is verified by a follow-up audit. Such audits are usually limited in scope to only verifying the corrective-action implementation. The effectiveness of the corrective action can be assessed in the same follow-up audit or in another follow-up. Alternatively, the effectiveness can be reviewed during the next regularly scheduled audit of that topic or area. In any case, the implementation (not the effectiveness) of the corrective action must not wait long. Five weeks or less is the most acceptable.

Follow-up audits may be conducted by the same auditor, an audit team leader, or a different auditor entirely, depending on what the audit procedure for the company requires.

The same corrective action showing up over and over again in the same place indicates that the corrective action is ineffective. A new and different corrective action that gets to the root cause needs to be implemented. The same corrective-action response coming from different parts of the quality system and different auditees may indicate a cultural problem within the company. Analysis of corrective-action patterns can give some insight into a company's real attitudes and philosophy that may not be the same as what the auditees would like to present. This is especially applicable when auditing suppliers.

CHAPTER 9

Auditor Training

The amount and type of training an auditor should have depends on the situation. A person who will be auditing other companies to determine whether or not they should be ISO 9000 certified requires a different level of training than someone who is one of several internal auditors of an already ISO 9000 certified company. A person doing supplier surveys for a non-ISO 9000 company may have a different background and still perform well. It all depends on who the auditor works for, the purpose of the audit, and the kind of audit being performed. In any situation, the auditor should be a good communicator, listener, and observer and be financially and emotionally neutral to the auditee.

The level of training and types of knowledge an auditor needs depends on what is being audited and why. Someone performing supplier audits must be familiar with the needs of the employer and the supplier's quality history. It helps to be familiar with the supplier's products and processes as well as the audit questions. If the audit is being done to find the root cause of a problem, then technical knowledge and powers of observation may be more important than actual auditing skill. Auditors doing an attribute-style audit from a yes/no checklist for the purpose of identifying a prospective vendor's abilities need only to be able to follow the checklist, and recognize and collect evidence. They should also have some technical background.

Internal auditors who audit their own employer's ISO 9000 systems should be trained specifically for this. Training usually takes three to five days, depending on the level of training to be given. A least one person should be designated as the company's lead auditor and should be trained as ISO 9000 certified. This is a weeklong training program. The other internal auditors do not all need this same level of training. There are companies that do a three-day training program where the auditors are trained in ISO 9000 on the first day, auditing techniques on the second day, and the third day is a supervised training audit. An additional day of training is usually given before this supervised audit if the training is for QS 9000 audits.

Besides these training programs, the American Society for Quality (formerly A.S.Q.C.) offers training in quality auditing. After the auditor finishes the course an exam can be taken and, if the auditor's score is high enough, the A.S.Q.C.

will certify the person as a Certified Quality Auditor (C.Q.A.). Automotive Industry Action Group (A.I.A.G.) and some private industrial training companies offer courses in QS 9000.

Any one of these training programs is good training for internal quality auditing, but they are not equal. If an auditor has ISO 9000 auditor training that goes beyond being a certified auditor and has worked with registered auditors, the auditor may eventually become a *registered* ISO 9000 auditor. This enables the auditor to work with a registrar to evaluate other companies for the purpose of determining their ISO 9000 registration qualification.

Regardless of the type of training given a new auditor, the value of working with an experienced auditor cannot be overstated. It is very important that new auditors accompany experienced auditors at least once, perhaps several times. All auditors being trained should also be given some training on conducting the audit interviews and using any checklist or audit forms necessary.

Sample Audit Forms

A-1. *Audit Checklist*

Audit Type	Internal	Supplier	Other (explain)	Date
Topic/Scope of Audit:				
Location of Audit:				
Responsible Manager for Audit Area:				
Other Contacts:				
Auditor(s):				

Question	Notes	Compliance
1.		
2.		
3.		
4.		
5.		
6.		
7.		
8.		

A-2. *Audit Noncompliance Form*

Audit date:	System/manual Section:	Auditor(s)
Topic/Scope of Audit:		
Location of Audit:		
Responsible Manager for Audit Area:		
Other Contacts:		

Description of Specific Noncompliance Found:

Auditor(s) Signature(s)	Responsible Manager's Signature

Description of Specific Noncompliance Found:

Corrective Action Due Date:	Follow-up Audit Due Date:

Follow-up Audit Results:

Corrective Action Satisfactorily Completed:	Yes	No
Further Follow-up Needed:	Yes	No
Further Follow-up/Comments:		

	Signature of Closing Auditor:

A-3. *Attribute Audit Checklist*

Audit Type	Internal	Supplier	Other (explain)	Date
Topic/Scope of Audit:				
Location of Audit:				
Responsible Manager for Audit Area:				
Other Contacts:				
Auditor(s):				

Question	N/A	Yes	No
1.			
2.			
3.			
4.			
5.			
6.			
7.			
8.			

A-4. *Audit Schedule and Record of Completion*

Month	Elements/Sections to be Audited	Auditor(s)	Contact(s)	Start Date	Completion Date

A-5. *Internal Auditor Training Record*

Auditor Name	Department	Supervisor	Date Training Completed	Trainer
1. _____	_____	_____	_____	_____
2. _____	_____	_____	_____	_____
3. _____	_____	_____	_____	_____
4. _____	_____	_____	_____	_____
5. _____	_____	_____	_____	_____
6. _____	_____	_____	_____	_____
7. _____	_____	_____	_____	_____
8. _____	_____	_____	_____	_____
9. _____	_____	_____	_____	_____
10. _____	_____	_____	_____	_____

Glossary

Activity The implementation and documentation comprising a single aspect or function of the entire quality system.

Attribute audits A type of audit where the questions are answered with either yes or no without score or evaluation. Such audits are pass/fail in nature.

Audit The examination of policies, procedures, and instructions, their implementation, performance, results, and records.

Auditee The person or persons being audited. The auditee is usually responsible for carrying out the policies, procedures, and instructions, and maintaining records of the results.

Auditor The person conducting the audit, doing the examining.

Compliance The status where the purpose and content of a document or activity supports the purpose and implements the content of the written documentation authorizing or requiring it.

Conformance Often used as a synonym for compliance, though it more properly applies to characteristics of objects than to documents and activities.

Corrective action Actions carried out to correct a noncompliance.

Evidence Records, artifacts, and physical characteristics proving that the items audited were in fact examined and either were or were not properly carried out.

Follow-up An audit of corrective action initiated by a previous audit.

Instruction A document that tells how an activity is to be performed or a policy implemented.

Internal Taking place entirely within a company and performed only by company employees.

Interdisciplinary Involving more than one field of knowledge and consequently usually more than one department.

ISO 9001　　　　An international standard describing the requirements for an interdisciplinary quality system and its relation to management and nonquality departments.

Noncompliance　An observation or evidence indicating that an activity or document does not meet the intent or proper implementation of a policy, procedure, or instruction.

Nonconformance　Often used as a synonym for noncompliance. *See also* conformance.

Policy　　　　　A document that describes the company's goal and attitude.

Procedure　　　A document that describes who does what, when, and often where, so as to implement a policy.

QS-9000　　　　A standard containing the entirety of ISO 9001, but adding requirements and information specific to U.S. automotive companies (now being adopted internationally).

Record　　　　Documentation, either hardcopy or recorded, on any media that proves an activity has taken place. Physical objects used as records are called retains.

Registrar　　　The authorized organization that can audit and register a company as being compliant with ISO 9001 or QS 9000.

Also called the R.A.B. When registered, a company receives a certificate attesting to the compliance.

Report   Documentation indicating the completion of an audit including the results, evidence, and documentation of any noncompliance.

Score   The measure of merit of an activity given by an auditor after examining an activity. Audits that are scored often have a minimum score necessary to pass the audit. Usually used to evaluate a proposed supplier.